Books should be returned on or before the
last date stamped below

0 8 JAN 2007

- 1 OCT 2008

28. OCT 09.

26 JAN 2010

3 0 NOV 2011

0 1 OCT 2012

1 3 OCT 2012

1 7 NOV 2012

221113

2 3 OCT 2012

- 7 NOV 2017

- 6 NOV 2018

1 7 DEC 2018

SEASONS SEASONS SEASONS SEASONS

AUTUMN

Moira Butterfield

Illustrated by Helen James

W

FRANKLIN WATTS
LONDON • SYDNEY

 An Appleseed Editions book

First published in 2005 by Franklin Watts
96 Leonard Street, London EC2A 4XD

Franklin Watts Australia
Level 17/207 Kent Street, Sydney, NSW 2000

© 2005 Appleseed Editions

Designed and illustrated by Helen James
Edited by Mary-Jane Wilkins
Tree illustration page 24 Moira Butterfield

ISBN 0 7496 6002 3

A CIP catalogue for this book is available from the British Library

Photographs by Corbis (James L. Amos, KIN CHEUNG/Reuters, Anna Clopet,
John Conrad, Daniel J. Cox, Chinch Gryniewicz; Ecoscene, Chris Lisle,
Craig Tuttle, Larry Williams)

Printed and bound in Thailand

Contents

All about autumn

Autumn is a season when leaves change colour, the nights grow longer and the weather is cooler.

The sun gives us life. Without it there would be no animals or plants on our planet.

Our sun journey

Our Earth travels round the sun, a huge fiery ball of burning gas that gives us our heat and light. It takes one year for the Earth to journey all the way round.

Earth words

The two halves of the world are called the northern and the southern hemispheres. While one has autumn, the other has spring. The area around the middle of the world is called the equator.

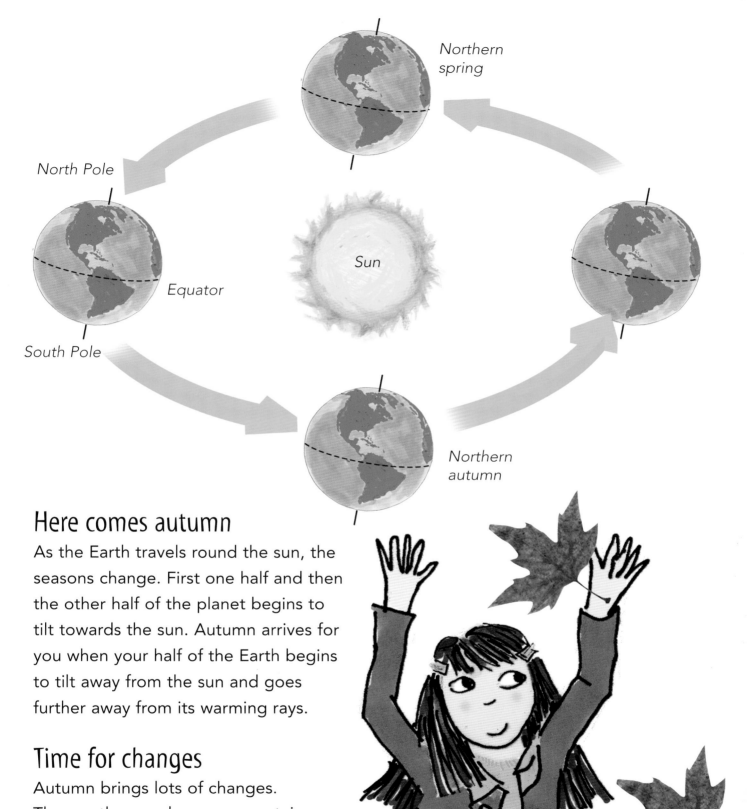

Northern
spring

North Pole

Equator

South Pole

Sun

Northern
autumn

Here comes autumn

As the Earth travels round the sun, the seasons change. First one half and then the other half of the planet begins to tilt towards the sun. Autumn arrives for you when your half of the Earth begins to tilt away from the sun and goes further away from its warming rays.

Time for changes

Autumn brings lots of changes. The weather can be very uncertain, but it gradually grows colder and colder, until finally winter comes.

5

My autumn, your autumn

Autumn comes at different times around the world. When it is autumn where you live, it is spring on the opposite side of the world.

Autumn north and south

In the northern half of the Earth autumn comes in September, October and November. In the southern half of the world autumn comes in March, April and May.

In the northern hemisphere the eastern USA is famous for the beautiful colours of its trees in autumn.

In the southern hemisphere, Antarctica is freezing and windy in the autumn.

The equator has wet and dry seasons.

What about the middle?

In countries along the equator it is hot all year round. There is no spring or autumn and places have wet and dry seasons instead.

Days and nights

As the Earth travels round the sun it spins in space like a top. It takes 24 hours to spin once. First one side faces the sun, then the other, giving us days and nights. In autumn the days grow shorter and the nights grow longer.

Autumn light show

In autumn you can see lights glowing in the night sky over countries in the far northern hemisphere. They are called the Northern Lights or the Aurora Borealis. Natural electricity flashes in the sky, creating the lights.

The colours of the Northern Lights glow and flash in the autumn sky over the countries of the far north.

The autumn brings darkness

The North and South Poles are in darkness for six months of the year, during the seasons of autumn and winter. When autumn arrives, the sun disappears from the sky. It won't return until spring.

Autumn's coming

When autumn arrives the natural world starts changing. Here are some autumn signs to look out for.

Above your head

As the weather grows cooler some tree leaves change colour and drop off. That's why autumn is called fall in America. It's often windy in autumn, and the wind helps to blow the dead leaves off the branches.

Under your feet

On the ground you might see nuts such as conkers that drop from trees and bushes. Your feet might crunch over fallen leaves and you might spot fungi such as mushrooms that grow at this time of year.

Chillier times

You can feel autumn coming when the temperature drops outside. We measure temperature with a thermometer that has coloured liquid inside. The liquid squeezes up a thin tube as it grows warmer, and drops lower in the tube when it grows colder. Numbers along the tube measure how far up the liquid goes.

These numbers show the temperature, measured in degrees Celsius (°C) or degrees Fahrenheit (°F).

Sunny, windy or wet?

In autumn the weather can be very changeable. One day it might be sunny and still. The next day it could be windy and wet!

9

Autumn weather

Autumn can be very windy! It can also be a damp season when you see mists and dew.

Why is it windy?

Wind is air moving around in the sky. Winds blow when warm air rises up and cold air rushes in to fill the space underneath. In autumn the air becomes cooler, and this creates air movement.

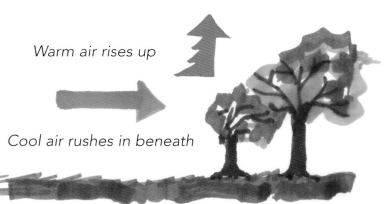

Warm air rises up

Cool air rushes in beneath

Windmills

Wind was once used to power windmills which ground corn into flour. Grinding equipment inside worked when the windmill sails turned.

World's windiest place

Antarctica is the windiest place in the world. Autumn is the windiest season there, when tearing hurricanes (very strong winds) blow across the snow.

Power from the wind

Wind is used to turn wind farm propellers. As they spin around they make electricity.

Foggy days

Autumn can be a foggy time. Fog appears when the air cools. Tiny particles of water in the air condense, which means they turn into mist that you can see. A fog is a very thick mist.

Drops of dew hang on a cobweb like tiny diamonds.

Dewy days

When water vapour condenses near the ground it settles on cold surfaces, such as grass stalks. This is dew and it appears early in the morning. It disappears as the day grows warmer.

Autumn garden

In the autumn leaves cover the ground and plants drop seeds, some inside juicy fruits or crunchy nuts.

All about leaves

Trees that lose their leaves in the autumn are called deciduous trees. Trees that keep their leaves all year round are called evergreen trees. This is why deciduous tree leaves change colour and die.

1. Plant leaves take a gas called carbon dioxide from the air and suck up water from the soil. They use sunlight to make these into food.

4. The leaves die and fall off because they are no longer needed for making food. New ones grow again in spring.

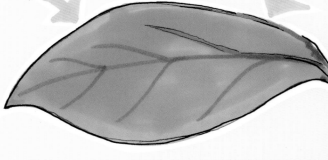

2. Leaves contain chlorophyll, a green substance that absorbs (soaks up) the sunlight the plant needs to make its food.

3. In autumn and winter plants stop making food. They don't need chlorophyll, so it disappears. That's why leaves change colour.

Red, yellow, brown and orange

Autumn leaves can be different colours even though they are on the same tree. This is because the chemicals inside each leaf change differently. The changes depend on the weather and the sunlight.

Fruits and seeds

Plants make seeds. Sometimes they are surrounded by fruit to protect them. Pea pods, berries and nuts are all fruits with seeds inside. The seeds drop and land in a new spot where they can grow.

All sorts of seeds

Some seeds are shaped like flat wings so they can glide on the wind. Some are hidden inside a tasty fruit or nut to tempt animals to carry them away. Some plants have seed heads that burst open and fling out all the seeds.

A dandelion head has lots of tiny seeds that blow away on the wind.

Autumn farm

Autumn is a busy time on farms that grow crops. The harvest must be brought in before the weather grows really cold and spoils the plants.

Time to pick grapes

In wine-growing parts of the world, autumn is the season for picking ripe grapes from the vines. They are ready to make into wine. In France this harvest is called the vendange. Once all the grapes are picked the farmers usually celebrate with a special party for all the pickers.

Grapes are picked to make wine and grape juice.

Beating the weather

Farmers must keep an eye on the autumn weather because they can only harvest crops during dry spells. They often work day and night to bring in the harvest quickly. Some crops are sold. Some are stored in barns to feed animals during winter.

Crops are stored away safely for the winter.

Secret smelly harvest

Many different crops are harvested in autumn. In southern Italy it's time to harvest the world's most expensive food, a rare and tasty fungus called the white truffle.

Truffles grow underground in woods. The best places to find them are kept secret. The truffle-hunters use trained pigs or dogs to sniff out where they are buried. They hunt for the truffles at night, when the fungus smells strongest.

A trained truffle pig looks for a rare white truffle.

15

Animals in the autumn

For many animals autumn is the time to prepare for the winter ahead, when it will be cold and hard to find food.

Collecting dinner

The woodland floor is scattered with nuts and seeds at this time of year. Woodland rodents such as squirrels and mice eat as much as they can to fatten up. They also collect food to store in their burrows during winter.

Getting cosy

Some animals hibernate during winter, which means they sleep inside a den until spring. Autumn is the time to prepare the den.

A badger gets a burrow ready for winter. It takes dry leaves and grass inside to sleep on.

Fat means survival

Many animals go without food when it is hard to find during winter. They survive by using the fat in their bodies to make energy. This is why they eat as much as they can in the autumn, to fatten up.

In Antarctica, in the far south, Emperor penguins eat as much fish as they can during autumn, to make themselves fat. They have to survive without food through the world's worst winters.

A warm coat

Many furry animals begin to grow a thicker coat in the autumn. The extra fur will help to keep them warm when winter arrives.

This Arctic fox has grown a thicker coat to keep it warm through the coming winter.

Autumn journeys

Many creatures migrate in the autumn, which means they make a journey to a new home to find food and better weather. They will return in spring.

Birds and butterflies

As the sun grows weaker in autumn more and more animals sense the cold and start moving. The skies fill with birds, butterflies and dragonflies travelling to their winter home. Some birds can sleep as they fly on long journeys. Their wings keep flapping as they take short naps.

Underwater journeys

Sea animals make autumn journeys too. Spiny lobsters spend the summer off the coast of Florida, USA. In the autumn they journey to deeper, less stormy waters. Lines of up to 50 lobsters march along the seabed together, each lobster touching the one in front.

Following the food

In the autumn tiny creatures called plankton swim away from the stormy sea surface. They go deeper and move to warmer waters. Shrimp-like animals called krill follow the plankton to eat them. Krill-eating whales follow, too.

The longest trip

A little bird called the Arctic tern makes the longest migration of all. In September, when autumn arrives in the Arctic, terns leave the far north and fly all the way around the world to the Antarctic. The following June, they fly all the way back again!

Autumn stories

All over the world people have stories about autumn. Here are two of them.

The moon goddess

This story is told at the Chinese Moon Festival in autumn, held at the time of year when the moon is at its brightest and fullest.

Once, many years ago, ten suns appeared in the sky. The Earth began to burn up and the crops to die, so the Chinese emperor commanded his best archer to shoot down nine of the suns. The archer was called Hou Yi and his wife was a beautiful lady called Chang-o.

Hou Yi shot down nine of the suns and as a reward he was given a magic pill that would make him live forever.

"Think long and hard before you take this pill. You must prepare yourself," he was told, so he took it home and hid it while he thought about how to prepare himself.

One day, while Hou Yi was away his wife found the pill and ate it. She instantly flew to the moon, where she still lives in a crystal palace. Her husband visits her, at the time of the moon festival, when she is at her most beautiful.

Spacecraft lanterns made for the Chinese Moon Festival in Hong Kong.

Anansi and the wind

In the Caribbean people tell their children many old stories about Anansi the spider-man.

Anansi had a large tree in his garden and every year he waited excitedly for the fruit to ripen. One year, when the fruit was still unripe, the wind came and blew it all off the tree. Anansi shouted at the wind.

"You destroyed my crop. What can I feed my family?" he raged.

"Oops, sorry," said the wind. "Take this magic tablecloth and when you feel hungry just say 'Spread, cloth, spread'. It will fill with food."

This worked very well until one day somebody in Anansi's house washed the magic tablecloth. After that it didn't work, so Anansi stomped over to where the wind lived and shouted at the wind again.

"This tablecloth is rubbish! Do something about it!" he cried.

"That's strange," the wind said, puzzled. "You'd better take this magic cooking pot instead. Say 'Cook, pot, cook' and it will fill with food."

This worked very well until somebody in Anansi's house cleaned the magic cooking pot. After that it didn't work, so Anansi stormed back to the wind's house and tried to boss the wind about.

"You've got to sort this out," he ordered.

"Nobody bosses me about like this," the wind muttered and he decided to teach Anansi a lesson. "Take this magic stick," he said. "Whenever you want something just say, 'Come on, stick!'"

When Anansi got hungry again he said, "Come on, stick!", but this time no food appeared. Instead the stick jumped up and chased him into the river!

Autumn parties

Lots of people celebrate autumn with parties.
Here are some of them.

Thanks for food

In the USA Thanksgiving is celebrated in autumn. People eat a turkey dinner like the one the pilgrims (the first European settlers) ate after their first harvest. They ate wild turkey with corn, sweet potatoes, nuts, berries and pumpkin.

22

Harvest festivals

There are lots of harvest parties around the world in autumn. In European Christian countries people bring fruit, vegetables and loaves to church to celebrate harvest festival. In Ghana, Africa, the Ewe people celebrate their yam harvest with drumming and dancing.

Inuit tug-of-war

In the far north of Canada the Inuit people celebrate autumn with a tug-of-war. They have two teams   the ducks (people born in warm months) and the ptarmigans (people born in cold months). If the ducks win, it is a sign that the coming winter will be mild. If the ptarmigans win, it's a sign that the coming winter is going to be a very cold one.

Spooky Halloween

Halloween falls on 31 October in northern lands. There are lots of superstitions (old beliefs) connected with this night, which people once thought marked the beginning of winter. They thought that spooks and spirits came out on Halloween. People still make pumpkin lanterns for fun on Halloween night. They once believed the lanterns scared away the spooks.

Paint the autumn

Here are some ideas for making autumn pictures.

Make your picture glow

Think of the colours of autumn leaves and use them in your autumn pictures. Try brown, red, orange and golden yellow. They are called warm colours, because they remind people of fire.

Blow an autumn tree

Use a drinking straw to blow paint around and create a glowing autumn tree. You will need a drinking straw, some watery paint, paper and a paintbrush.

1. Paint a dark-coloured trunk using thick watery paint. Blow some of the paint up from the trunk to make branches.

2. Add different colours, one by one, blowing them around to make a mass of spiky autumn leaves.

Wax and scratch

Here is a way to make a picture of glowing fireworks or a bonfire on a dark autumn night. You will need wax crayons, black poster paint, a sharp-ended paintbrush and some newspaper.

1. Put the newspaper under your picture, because wax and scratching is quite messy.

2. Cover a piece of paper with thick lines of wax crayon. Try diagonal red and yellow for fire, or stripes of several colours for fireworks.

3. Cover the whole of the paper with the poster paint. When it's dry paint another layer to make it thick.

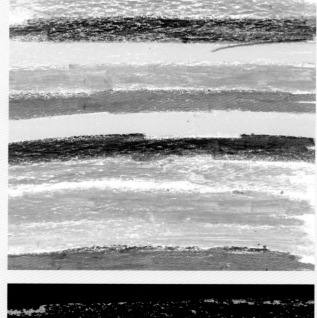

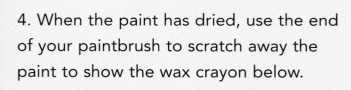

4. When the paint has dried, use the end of your paintbrush to scratch away the paint to show the wax crayon below.

Make a piece of autumn

Make some wood people puppets from autumn leaves, and a mini spinning windmill.

Wood people puppets

Go for a woodland walk on a dry day and take a plastic bag. Collect some dry leaves and twigs. You will also need stiff thick card, scissors, glue, sticky tape and felt-tips or paint.

1. Cut out a body shape from card, about as tall as two big leaves.

2. Coat the body with glue. Stick on big leaves to make a skirt, and small ones to make sleeves and hair. Leave the puppet to dry overnight.

A shape with a wide skirt

3. When the puppet is dry, tape a twig across the back to make arms. Tape a thick stick down the back, so you can hold your puppet.

Windmill

To make this wind toy you will need two squares of sticky-backed paper in two different colours, glue, scissors, a ruler, a strong drinking straw and a drawing pin.

1. Stick the two pieces of paper back to back so that the edges match.

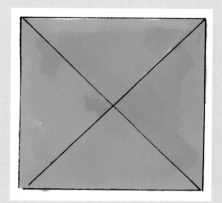 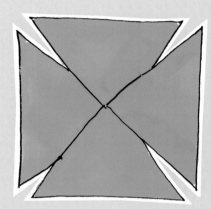

2. Fold the square diagonally twice, to make crease marks in the shape of an X.

3. Use your ruler to measure and mark half way along each part of the X. Then cut in to the marks from the points of the square.

4. Fold every other point into the middle and glue them down.

5. Push the drawing pin through the middle and into the top of the straw. Then blow the windmill to make sure it spins.

Be an autumn scientist

Discover some autumn science by finding out what the wind carries, and the secret of moving air.

Catch things on the wind

You will need a paper picnic plate, some string, some petroleum jelly, scissors and a magnifying glass.

1. Ask an adult to punch a hole in the picnic plate so that you can hang it up with the string.

2. Smear the petroleum jelly over one side of the plate.

3. Hang it outside for an hour or so on a dry windy day.

4. Bring it in and use your magnifying glass to see what the wind has blown on to your plate. You might have insects, dust, bits of grass or seeds.

The secret of moving air

Air moves when it warms up. You can test this by making a spiral mobile.
You will need some thick paper, a dinner plate to draw round, a pencil,
scissors, string. Test your mobile over a central-heating radiator.

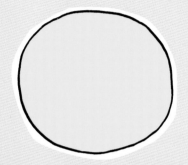

1. Draw round the plate to make a circle
on the paper. Draw a spiral inside the
circle and decorate it with stripes, or
to look like a wriggly snake.

2. Cut round the circle and the spiral.

3. Ask an adult to help you thread the
string through the middle. Pull the paper
gently downwards so that the spiral
stretches out.

4. Hang the spiral high above the top
of the radiator. Then leave it
to see what happens.

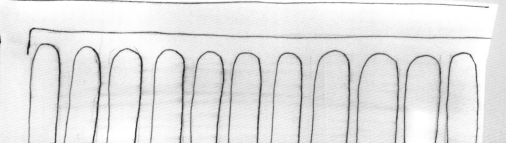

The air above the radiator
is warmed. It rises up and
makes the spiral spin. Wind
is caused by warm air rising
up, and cold air rushing
into the space underneath.

Words to remember

chlorophyll A green substance in leaves. It soaks up sunlight to help plants make food.

crops Plants that farmers grow and harvest.

deciduous tree A tree that loses its leaves in winter. The leaves change colour and begin to die in autumn.

dew Water that comes out of the air and settles on the ground.

evergreen tree A tree that does not lose its leaves in winter.

fog A thick mist hanging in the air.

fruit A layer that grows round a seed to protect it.

fungi A kind of plant that does not have leaves. – ushrooms and toadstools are fungi. They often grow in autumn.

hemispheres The northern and the southern halves of the world.

migration A seasonal journey that animals make from one home to another, to find more food and warmer weather.

Northern Lights Flashing lights that appear in the skies of the far north. They are strong during autumn.

season A time of year that has a particular kind of weather and temperature.

seed A little package containing all the things needed for a new plant to grow.

temperature How hot or cold something is.

thermometer A tube with liquid inside that is used to measure temperature.

water vapour Tiny drops of water floating in the air, so small you can't see them.

wind Air moving around.

Index